Strategic Planning

A Brief Guideline

Ursina Teuscher, PhD

Content

What Is Strategic Planning?

Strategic planning is an organization's process of defining its direction and deciding on how to pursue it.

Strategy involves fundamental choices about organizational direction.

Planning involves setting goals, determining actionable steps to achieve the goals, and mobilizing resources to execute the plan.

As a comprehensive process, it can include many components.

An essential first step is to clarify the mission, vision and values of an organization. Tightly linked to this is a clear understanding of the different kinds of stakeholders: what their needs are, and how they benefit from and contribute to your organization.

Based on this fundamental understanding of your organization's role and purpose, next steps are to appraise the business' full potential and opportunities, along with the constraints and organizational needs.

All this will inform an exploration and evaluation of possible strategies. Once you have decided on a strategy, you can define specific goals, both for the short and long term. You can plan courses of action to achieve those goals, monitor the progress, and establish a process to re-evaluate and adjust.

Why Is It Important?

Strategic Planning offers a systematic process to address the most critical questions confronting an organization—especially large, irrevocable resource commitment decisions.

It helps decision makers be proactive in looking for opportunities, rather than reacting to problems.

Where a team is involved, the process has at least three additional important benefits.

First, it builds engagement and commitment. It increases the team members' confidence in the organization's direction and gives everyone an understanding of a shared focus.

Second, it encourages fact-based discussions of politically sensitive issues. As an example, it can set a proper context for budget decisions and performance evaluations.

Third, and perhaps most importantly, it empowers group members to make their own decisions on a continuing basis. A sound strategic plan creates a common framework for decision-making in the organization and can be the basis for specific guidelines for employees' daily decisions.

When Should Strategic Planning Happen?

There is never a wrong moment for strategic planning, because it will inform not only your current decisions, but will help you look for decision opportunities that you might otherwise miss.

That said, there are times and situations in which strategic planning is particularly important and useful.

Obvious moments are those when your organization is undergoing or facing big changes, which require big decisions. For example, sudden growth, new sources of funding, or on the other end financial straights or new competitors might lead you to think about new strategies.

In other words, you may have new opportunities, or new problems, which require thinking and planning.

Other great moments for planning are those when you have new data, such as customer reviews.

You may also want to take a step back to rethink your direction when new people are joining your team who will be major decision makers.

Aside from those triggers, it is a good idea to schedule strategic planning as a repeating event, for example in the form of an annual facilitated team retreat.

If you are the sole decision maker in your organization, for example if you are self-employed or a small business owner, regular strategic planning can happen in the form of coaching or consulting sessions, but also in the form of a yearly more intense session.

What Elements Are Included?

The upcoming sections describe the following building blocks of an effective strategic plan:

1. **Mission, Vision, Values**
2. **Stakeholder Analysis**
3. **SWOT Analysis**
4. **Exploring Strategies**
5. **Deciding on Strategies**
6. **Setting Major Goals**
7. **Strategic Action Planning**

As a general guideline, it makes sense to tackle each of those steps in the sequence in which they are presented here. However, depending on your organization's history and situation, some sections may require more focus than others. As an example, if you are having yearly strategic planning sessions, there may be no need to work in depth on the mission statement every time – it may be enough to just reconfirm whether everybody is still on board with it.

1. Mission, Vision, Values

Mission Statement

Why We Exist

The mission statement is the compass in the storm of organizational life. It is a statement of purpose of the organization. It may be a short sentence, but it should spell out the organization's overall goal and have the potential to guide decisions and actions. It provides the framework within which the company's strategies are formulated.

The mission statement gives an answer to the following essential questions:

Why do we exist as an organization?

and

What do we do for Whom?

Other ways to get to the bottom of this are to ask:

What is our cause – the purpose for our existence?
What gap do we fill? How do we make difference?
Why should people care about what we do?

The "**Why**" should be the first question, but it is tightly linked to the question of "**What** do we do for **Whom**?"

In as few words as possible, the mission statement should describe the core outcome, such as a service or product, and the people for whom it will make a difference. If you are truly filling a gap, this is your *unique value contribution*.

Note that in some cases, for example for non-profit organizations, the people receiving the services or products may not be the same people as those who are paying for the services or products. It is crucial to think about the needs of both those groups and how the organization contributes value to both of them. The section *Stakeholder Analysis* (starting on page 15) will discuss this topic in more depth, but the mission statement should already make clear who benefits most from the work of the organization.

The mission statement should be written as succinctly as possible. It should not include any specifics about methods or technology, unless those are essential in filling a gap.
It is important to keep the statement in simple terms, so it can easily be understood and talked about in an informal conversation. Every member of the organization should be able to comfortably and naturally say it to any outside person, in any social context, and enjoy talking about it.

"What is well conceived is spoken clearly,
And the words to say it flow with ease."
Nicolas Boileau-Despréaux

Test yourself, once you have written it. Try your mission statement at the next social opportunity, such as a party or family gathering. You should be excited and comfortable talking about your mission, and the words should flow easily, from your heart.

Vision Statement

Where We Are Headed

The vision statement is directed to the future. It describes a **desired end state** – an inspirational long-term change that you want to result from your work.

The vision statement gives an answer to the question:

What will be different if we are successful?

When developing a vision statement, imagine a dream end state in the longer-term future.

An effective vision statement creates a mental image of a future state that the organization wants to achieve. It is aspirational and inspirational – it should challenge and motivate your members.
The vision can be utopian, describing a world in which all your goals were achieved. However, while your vision may describe an unlikely ideal, it should follow logically from your mission statement – it is the state that would result if your mission were accomplished to perfection.

On the next page are some examples of famous mission and vision statements. Note in those examples how the vision – even though it describes a utopian, rather than realistic state, follows directly from the mission.

As you craft your mission statement, you may also consider starting out with your vision statement to lead into your mission statement, along these lines:

> *"Our vision is a community where _____. To bring that into reality, we do _____."*

You can expand on the practical part of your mission statement by further describing what you do, for whom, and where.

> *"Our vision is a community where _____. To bring that into reality, we do _____ for _____ in _____."*

Examples of Mission and Vision Statements

Feeding America

Mission:
Our mission is to feed America's hungry through a nationwide network of member food banks and engage our country in the fight to end hunger.

Vision:
Creating a hunger-free America.

Kiva

Mission:
We are a non-profit organization with a mission to connect people through lending to alleviate poverty.

Vision:
We envision a world where all people – even in the most remote areas of the globe – hold the power to create opportunity for themselves and others.

Habitat for Humanity International

Mission:
Habitat for Humanity brings people together to build homes, communities and hope.

Vision:
A world where everyone has a decent place to live.

Values Statement

What We Stand For

Values are the principles that guide the organization's day-to-day decisions.

An effective value statement therefore has very practical applications. It specifies the core priorities of the organizational culture, in line with the ideals defined in your mission and vision.

The values statement gives an answer to the question:

What principles guide the way we work and make decisions?

Within the trio of mission, vision and values, the values statement is perhaps the most under-rated. A well-written values statement is a very practical tool. It can guide the decisions of the organization as a whole, as well as those of its members. It tells the world outside and inside the organization what you are committing to. By defining your priorities, the values statement helps you make tough decisions as they come along. It is a tool by which you can measure whether or not you are indeed walking the talk.

To define your values, it is a good idea to first look outside the organization, to the visionary outcomes you want to create in your community.

What values would have to be the norm in your community so that your vision could become a reality?

From there, you can look inside and define how your own work will model those values.

How do you ensure you are teaching those values by example?

Whenever you face tough decisions, how will you choose the courses of actions that are most aligned with those values?

Without a values-based context for decision-making, groups are more likely to default to fear-based decisions when things get tough. It is a great defense against making fear-based or other impulsive decisions to have discussed core values ahead of time.

Application: The Trio in Practice

At one of your next meetings in your organization, such as a board meeting, use your three statements to do a quick self-evaluation.

1. Vision

Have we done our work in a way that will move our vision forward? How might we change our work to aim at that vision?

2. Mission

Have we done our work in a way that is accomplishing our mission? How might we change our work to ensure we are accomplishing that work?

3. Values

Have we done our work in a way that adheres to our shared core values? How might we change our work to ensure we are indeed walking our talk?

2. Stakeholder Analysis

Identifying Stakeholders

A stakeholder is anybody who is affected by or can affect your organization. You can think of stakeholders in terms of groups of people, as well as in terms of important individuals.

Some typical *internal stakeholders* could be employees, managers, owners, or board members.

External stakeholders could be clients, investors, funding agencies, the government, vendors, suppliers, fans, or any member of society who has an interest for or against your mission. Less obvious groups of stakeholders might, for example, include families of employees, or friends of clients.

The first step in a stakeholder analysis is to identify your *current stakeholders*.

Who is affected by your decisions?
Who cares about your organization?

Make a list of everybody you can think of who is, or will be, affected by your organization.

Then, think about *potential stakeholders*: people who might become your stakeholders if something were different about your organization – for example: if they knew about you; if you targeted different clients; if you went international, etc.

Who else might be your stakeholders?
Who else might care about you if ...?

A simple brainstorming activity is a good way for this first step of identifying as many stakeholders as possible. If you are doing this in a group, give everyone a block of sticky notes and ask them to write every name, organization or type of stakeholder they can think of on a note.

Hold on to those sticky notes for the exercise of prioritizing stakeholders later on.

Considering Contributions by Stakeholders

Once you have identified your stakeholders, you want to think more specifically about each of their contributions.

Why do you care about your stakeholders?

Ask yourself what your different groups of stakeholders are contributing to your organization. Different stakeholders may provide different kinds of values. What are they currently willing to do for you?

For example, your clients or donors are willing to give you money. Other people, such as employees, board members, volunteers, are willing to give you their time and energy to work for you. Your fans, social media followers, or other supporters may be willing to recommend you, thereby giving you their trust by risking some of their own reputation if you fail.

Considering Interests of Stakeholders

Then, turn the question around and ask yourself how each group of stakeholders can benefit most from your organization.

Why do your stakeholders care about you?

Your different stakeholders may have different priorities and expectations to you.

For example, what are your clients or donors willing to pay for? Why are some people willing to give you their time? What are they willing to work for? Why would some people put their own reputation on the line in order to recommend you?

For each group, also ask yourself under what circumstances they might be willing to do even more.

Prioritizing Stakeholders

If the process of identifying stakeholders results in a long list of individuals and groups, you need to prioritize them in order of importance, since you can't fulfill all of their interests. You can do this by mapping the contributions and interests of each stakeholder group on four quadrants as shown in the template below.

	Interest Low	*Interest High*
Contribution High	... ... **= Supporters:** Can we increase their interest (move right)? Meet their needs? Engage and consult?	... ... **= Key Players:** How do we meet their needs? How do we keep them engaged?
Contribution Low	... ... **= Least Important:** Can we let them go? Keep them informed? Or is it worth trying to increase their interest *and* contribution (move up *and* right)?	... ... **= Potential Supporters:** Can we increase their contribution (move up)? Make use of their interest?

If you have worked with sticky notes to identify stakeholders as described on page 15, now is the time to put all those up on the wall. Draw the four quadrants on a flipchart and ask everyone to place their sticky notes into the quadrants they belong. If not everyone agrees in which quadrant different stakeholders belong, this will likely result in an important discussion in itself.

Once you have mapped out your stakeholders that way, you can decide how to focus your efforts. While you want to focus your strategies on the top right quadrant and do everything to keep your key players engaged, you'll also want to think about strategies that could increase the interest of those who are already contributing, and about strategies that could increase the contributions of those with the highest interest. If you are currently spending a lot of time, money or energy on stakeholders in the least important category, make a conscious decision of whether (and how) to let go of them, or whether to try increasing both their interests and contributions.

3. SWOT Analysis

The tool of the SWOT analysis was originally proposed by Albert Humphrey in the 1960's and has in the meantime become a classic as far as planning tools go. The acronym stands for **S**trengths, **W**eaknesses, **O**pportunities and **T**hreats. A SWOT analysis thus explores answers to these four questions:

> *What are your organization's...*
> > *strengths?*
> > *weaknesses?*
> > *opportunities?*
> > *threats?*

The questions call attention to both positive and negative resources in two main categories:

1) Internal factors – the strengths and weaknesses internal to the organization

2) External factors – the opportunities and threats presented by the environment external to the organization

Used effectively, a SWOT analysis creates a helpful framework for further discussion of strategies. It reveals positive forces to build on and take advantage of, and potential problems that need to be recognized and possibly addressed.

To conduct a SWOT analysis, ask your group members to answer these simple questions: what are the strengths and weaknesses of your organization, and what are the opportunities and threats facing it?
Think about these, for example, with regard to your resources, competencies, credentials, processes, stakeholders, environment, market, and competition. The table shows some general questions in each SWOT category to prompt your analysis.

	Positives	Negatives
Internal, *e.g.:* *Capabilities* *Resources* *Processes* *Clients*	**Strengths** What are your advantages? What do you do well? What has led to successes so far? What unique resources can you draw on? What do others see as your strengths?	**Weaknesses** What could be improved in your organization? What resources or capabilities are you lacking? What do others likely see as your weaknesses?
External, *e.g.:* *Economy* *Competition* *Funding* *Legislation* *Technology*	**Opportunities** What possibilities are open to you, which could support or help your effort? Is an outside change favorable to your goal? What trends could you take advantage of?	**Threats** What obstacles do you face that hinder your effort? Is an outside change harmful to your goal? What is your competition doing?

Make four lists containing everybody's answers, one list each for strengths, weaknesses, opportunities and threats.

If you do this in a group setting, a facilitation method with sticky notes and flip charts works well. Ask people to brainstorm individually about these four questions and write each item on a sticky note.

Prepare four flip charts, each with one of these headings: "Strengths"; "Weaknesses"; "Opportunities"; and "Threats". Once everyone is done writing, each person will get up, state their items briefly for everyone to hear, and stick them on the charts.

There will most likely be overlap between the notes from different people. Therefore, as each person brings up their notes, ask them to group their sticky notes into distinct topics, in agreement with the previous sharers. Even after grouping the items to avoid redundancy, you may end up with long lists of factors at this point. If that is the case, prune and prioritize them, so that you spend your time thinking about the most significant factors.

A nice way to facilitate the prioritizing process in a group setting is to ask people to vote with colored stickers. You can hand out a number of sticker dots to each person, and ask them to place their dots next to the topics on the flipcharts they most care about. You will get an instant visual impression of which factors seem most important to most people.

Revisit the Mission Statement

After these last two steps of Stakeholder and SWOT analyses, it is a good idea to revisit the mission statement, hopefully only briefly. Does it still make sense in light of any new insights that came from these analyses? For example, the best mission statement in the world will be of little use if you have a competitor who does all of this better than you.

4. Exploring Strategies

Use your answers to the previous elements (the mission, vision and values statements, the stakeholder analysis, and the S.W.O.T. analysis) to inform your strategies.

Discuss each of the following questions with your group members:

*What strategies would **best fulfill your mission, vision and values**?*

*Which strategies would be best for your most important **stakeholders**?*

*Which strategies would take advantage of your **strengths**, minimize the impact your **weaknesses**, capitalize on your **opportunities**, and manage your **threats**?*

List all the possible options (strategies, courses of action) you can come up with.

Here are some examples of basic business strategies that may apply to your situation but that you'll need to specify:

- Expanding
- Contracting
- Staying liquid for future expansions
- Adding categories of your products or services
- Targeting different clients
- Narrowing your niche
- Differentiating yourself from competitors

The SWOT analysis described in the last section deserves a special focus here, because it prepares you to search in a very systematic way for strategies that take advantage of your strengths, minimize the impact your weaknesses, capitalize on your opportunities, and manage your threats.

In order to search for strategies based on your SWOT analysis, you match your opportunities and threats with your strengths and weaknesses, as illustrated in the matrix below.

First, copy the key conclusions from your SWOT analysis into the header cells of the table below. At this point, you'll want to focus only on the most important factors that came out of the SWOT analysis.

	Opportunities (O) 1. 2. 3. 4.	Threats (T) 1. 2. 3. 4.
Strengths (S) 1. 2. 3. 4.	SO Strategies: Use **strengths** to **maximize opportunities.**	ST Strategies: Use **strengths** to **minimize threats.**
Weaknesses (W) 1. 2. 3. 4.	WO Strategies: Take advantage of opportunities to **minimize weaknesses.**	WT Strategies: **Minimize or improve weaknesses** to **avoid threats.**

Now, look at each combination of internal and external factors and consider how you can use them to create good strategic options:

Strengths and Opportunities (SO)
How can you leverage your strengths to benefit from these opportunities?
How can you take advantage of opportunities that play into your strengths?

Strengths and Threats (ST)
How can you take advantage of your strengths to avoid real and potential threats?
How can you use your strengths to minimize the impact of threats?

Weaknesses and Opportunities (WO)
How can you use these opportunities to overcome your weaknesses?
How do you ensure your weaknesses will not deter you from opportunities?

Weaknesses and Threats (WT)
How can you avoid threats that are dangerous because of your weaknesses?
How can you improve weaknesses that would allow threats to have a real impact?

The options you identify are your strategic alternatives. List these in the appropriate quadrant.

Think Creatively About Your Strategies: Widen Your Options

Consider all the possible strategies you can see up to this point. What would be the best and worst aspects of each of your strategies?

Now – how can you come up with a better strategy that would combine the best parts of each, and have none (or fewer) of the drawbacks?

Amazingly often, we're able to come up with ideas that are much better than the first obvious solutions, just by thinking harder. Don't stop thinking too soon. Resist the urge to find a solution or agreement right away.

5. Deciding on Strategies

If at this point you have several strategies between which you need to decide, this section will equip you with a process and tools to evaluate them systematically.

Determine Criteria

First, determine your set of *criteria*, along which you want to evaluate your strategies.

This is where your values statement will come in handy. If you have a well thought out set of core values, those can immediately serve as your criteria to guide your decision. In addition to those, you may want to include criteria that matter specifically for your current situation.

Decision Table With Facts and Estimates

Once you have agreed on a set of criteria, organize your decision in the structure of a matrix, where the columns are your criteria, and the rows are your strategies. The table below shows this basic matrix structure and can serve as a template for your own decision table. Fill in your criteria as column headers, and your strategies as row headers. Then, fill each cell with your "data": what do you expect from each of your options, for each of your criteria?

	Criterion 1	Criterion 2	Criterion 3	Criterion ...
Strategy 1				
Strategy 2				
Strategy 3				
Strategy ...				

Such a table, filled with all the information and estimates you have about each strategy, creates a great deal of clarity even for very complex decisions. It allows you to integrate a lot of information and communicate clearly about issues without losing sight of the big picture.

If your decision is very controversial or impactful, you might consider asking outside experts to provide facts and estimates. This is also a great test: you know you have a well-defined set of criteria and strategies if an outside expert can complete the contents of this table for you.

Weighted Decision Table to Evaluate Strategies

Now you can use the same matrix structure for a quantitative analysis, to determine which of your possible strategies are winners. For that, determine the relative importance of each criterion, rate each option on each criterion, and calculate weighted totals for each strategy.

For example, give each cell a rating from 1 = worst to 10 = best, representing how much each criterion would benefit from each strategy. Then, multiply each weight with each raw rating, and add the weighted ratings up, in order to get a weighted total benefit for each strategy. The table below shows an example with numbers.

	Criterion 1	Criterion 2	Criterion 3	Total Benefit
Weights	30%	25%	45%	
Strategy 1	1	3	6	**3.75** (1*30%+3*25%+6*45%)
Strategy 2	2	5	9	**5.9** (2*30%+5*25%+9*45%)
Strategy 3	8	5	2	**4.55** (8*30%+5*25%+2*45%)

In this example, Strategy 2 is showing the greatest benefit, based on these weights and ratings.

This kind of quantitative table is easiest to work with in a spreadsheet, which you can project for everyone to see. But the calculations are simple enough that you can also work with the low-tech variant of drawing out the table on flip charts, and calculate the totals with a pocket calculator during a meeting.

In a group setting – whether you go high-tech or low-tech – there are two fundamentally different ways to decide on the weights and ratings: *consensus* or *democracy*. They both have their time and place.

A consensus is great, as long as it is genuine, rather than based on power inequalities or laziness. If you are aiming for a consensus, make sure there is room for objections being raised. Make an extra effort to solicit potentially differing opinions, and encourage people to play devil's advocates.
If your group can reach a consensus that way, you can fill in the weights and raw ratings together.

For a democratic process, where every person weighs in equally, make sure everyone hears all opinions before casting their votes.
If you are going for democracy, there are many ways to collect votes and aggregate them. For example, you can give everyone a copy of the decision table with the criteria and strategies you defined together, but with empty cells for weights and raw ratings. Have everyone fill in the weights and raw ratings, hand their copy in, and aggregate the results in a spreadsheet that you can present to the group. Or you can get a visual poll with sticky dots on a flip chart. Draw your decision table on a flip chart, again leaving the cells for weights and ratings empty. For the weights, hand out a the same number of colored sticky dots to each person, and ask them to distribute their dots along the criteria, giving more dots to the criteria that are more important to them. For the ratings, you can also work with sticky-dots in the same way, or you can ask each person to write their rating on a scale from 1 = worst to 10 = best into each cell, and calculate an average for each cell after everyone has voted.
If possible, do the voting procedure right before taking a break, so that you can calculate the results during the break and discuss them during the same meeting.

Sensitivity Analysis

If you were unsure about some of your ratings (perhaps because of unknown information, uncertain estimates, or because of disagreements in how much weight each criterion should get), you can test how robust a winner is. Simply play around with different weights and ratings and find out whether they make a difference in the final rank order.

When working with decision tables however, I am often surprised at the extent of agreement that results from this process, even for controversial topics, and between parties who had at first disagreed on the basis of an intuitive judgment. I believe that this amount of consensus is only possible because we start the process with defining criteria that everybody can identify with. This is crucial. Since we are working with a whole set of criteria, it is usually possible to get people on the same page about what matters. Even if group members disagree about specific criteria, they can often agree to the set as a whole, as long as their own priorities are represented. From there, the evaluation can go along very smoothly, because the process is transparent, is based on facts and estimates, and highlights winner strategies in a way that makes sense to everyone.

Improve the Winners

At this point it is worth giving some additional thought as to whether your winning strategies could be improved or combined in any way. The decision table helps you see which cells would need to be improved for any strategy to become a true win-win solution.

Note how the process of working with decision tables not only leads to more *agreement* than we would expect, even in diverse groups, but it also leads to a surprising amount of *innovation and creative thinking*, by drawing attention to features that have the potential of creating win-win strategies.

Cost-Benefit Analysis

If your strategies differ greatly in how much they will likely cost you (in terms of time, money, effort, risk, etc.), you can now easily add a *cost-benefit analysis* within the same matrix structure, as is shown in the table below.

You can copy the total benefits from your decision table above, and add a column with your estimated costs for each strategy. To calculate the cost-benefit ratio (CBR), you simply divide the estimated benefits by the estimated costs. The strategy with the smaller CBR is the better one.

CBR = Cost/Benefit
CBR > 1 is bad.
CBR < 1 is good.

	Total Estimated Benefit (from table above)	Total Estimated Cost	CBR: Cost/Benefit
Strategy 1			
Strategy 2			

Return on Investment

If you prefer, you can calculate a return on investment (ROI) instead of a CBR with the same ingredients. The ROI is defined as the gains from an investment minus the costs of it, divided by the costs. Or, as a formula:

ROI = (Gain from Investment - Cost of Investment)/Cost of Investment.

The CBR and the ROI therefore both give you fundamentally the same information, they just lead to opposite patterns in your rank order: the most effective strategies have the smallest CBR and the largest ROI.

Prepare to Be Wrong

Throughout this process, keep in mind that we are terrible at making predictions. Therefore, consider some or all the following, whatever is applicable to your situation:

- Give special weight to reversible options
- Have buffers and reserve
- Specify a "Plan B"
- Diversify
- Share risks
- Get expert opinions, but task them for information, rather than predictions, keeping in mind that experts are also poor predictors of the future.
- Plan on testing out your strategies in small steps
- Specify "trip-wires" that should initiate a change of plans

6. Major Goals

Once you're clear on your strategies, you can establish *major goals* for your next planning cycle. Define what changes you want to accomplish in what time frame.

The time frame of your next planning cycle will depend on factors such as your industry, funding sources, and the history and current state of your organization. A common time frame for long-term goals is a three to five year planning cycle. However if you are in a fast-changing market, one to three years might be all you can realistically plan for.

Major goals provide the framework for the next step: *strategic action plans*.

7. Strategic Action Plans

Strategic action plans identify specific pieces that will be required for the completion of each *major goal*. They provide a structure for fulfillment of those goals, consisting of specific projects and tasks.

Defining SMART Goals

The SMART acronym refers to five criteria for setting goals at this stage. SMART goals should be:
Specific
Measurable
Actionable
Realistic
Time-bound

Although the acronym has been used for other variations of similar words (such as "Attainable", "Results-based", etc.) the main purpose of framing action plans in line with these criteria is always to ensure accountability in terms of actions and outcomes.

For each of your *major goals* from the last section, define the next steps that are required to achieve them in terms of *SMART goals*, including deliverables and specific deadlines.

Assigning Roles and Responsibilities

If a team is involved, clearly define the roles and responsibilities for each SMART goal. A helpful tool for tracking roles and responsibilities is the Responsibility Assignment Matrix (RACI matrix). RACI stands for:

Who is...

    1) **R**esponsible?
    2) **A**ccountable?
    3) **C**onsulted?
    4) **I**nformed?

1) Responsible

Who is responsible for the execution of the task?

People in this role are the "doers": those who do the actual work that is required to achieve the goal. More than one person can be assigned to this role, as long their tasks are clear. Others can also be delegated to assist in the work.

2) Accountable

Who is accountable for the tasks and signs off the work?

The person in this role is also called "approver" or "final approving authority". He or she is the one ultimately answerable for the correct completion of the task, and the one who delegates the work to those responsible. In other words, an accountable must sign off on the completed deliverable. There must be only one accountable specified for each task.

3) Consulted

Who are experts who can or need to be consulted?

Those are also sometimes referred to as "counsel". They are typically subject matter experts, or otherwise people whose opinions matter, or whose advice may be helpful.

4) Informed

Who are the people who need to be updated on the progress?

Those are people who simply need to be kept in the loop. They receive updates on progress, maybe only upon completion of the task.

Example (Excerpt) of an Action Plan with Smart Goals and Assigned Deliverables:

Action Plan: Develop an Emergency Plan for the Clinic

SMART Goal: Ensure that patients requiring after-hours care have access to a secured service provider.

Task 1: Identify and contract with individuals in organization that can be after-hour service providers.

RACI: Who is...

Responsible:	Dave
Accountable:	Joan
Consulting:	Elizabeth
Informed:	Jade, Sam

Deliverable: Finished list of service providers, including our contact person with whom we contracted.

Deadline: 7/31

Task 2: Develop a set of emergency procedures (triage, contacts)

RACI: Who is...

Responsible:	Christina and Joan
Accountable:	Joan
Consulting:	Oscar
Informed:	All board members

Deliverable: Draft completed.

Deadline: 8/17

What Happens Next?

A strategic planning session should always end with scheduling.

Schedule follow-ups, where you monitor the progress on the action plan. If the tasks did not get done, figure out what the problems were and adapt.

Also schedule the next strategic planning session at a specific date, for example at the same time the following year. If this is a regular event, fundamental elements such as the mission statement may only be revisited briefly if there is continued agreement on them.

You may consider setting "trip wires" for additional strategic planning in between those sessions. For example, you may plan on reconvening in case of specific environmental changes or performance thresholds.

In between your planning sessions, always maintain the mindset to actively look for decision opportunities. Keep your criteria in mind and watch out for any additional opportunities to act in alignment with them and improve your strategies.

Selected References

3 Statements That Can Change the World: Mission / Vision / Values. Retrieved December 22, 2015, from http://www.help4nonprofits.com

About Feeding America. Retrieved December 22, 2015, from http://www.feedingamerica.org/about-us/about-feeding-america/

Brown, C. A. (1984). The Central Arizona Water Control Study: A Case for Multiobjective Planning and Public Involvement1. *JAWRA Journal of the American Water Resources Association*, 20(3), 331–337.

Anderson, B., Hahn, D., & Teuscher, U. (2013). *Heart and Mind: Mastering the Art of Decision Making*. CreateSpace Independent Publishing Platform.

Bryson, J. M. (2011). *Strategic Planning for Public and Nonprofit Organizations: A Guide to Strengthening and Sustaining Organizational Achievement* (4th Edition edition). San Francisco: John Wiley & Sons.

Community Tool Box. Retrieved December 22, 2015, from http://ctb.ku.edu/en

Drucker, Peter F. *Managing in a Time of Great Change*. Harvard Business Press, 2009.

Edwards, W., & von Winterfeldt, D. (1987). Public Values in Risk Debates. *Risk Analysis*, 7(2), 141–158.

Fawcett, S. B., Francisco, V. T., Schultz, J. A., Berkowitz, B., Wolff, T. J., & Nagy, G. (2000). The Community Tool Box: a Web-based resource for building healthier communities. *Public Health Reports*, 115(2-3), 274–278.

Freeman, R. E. (1984). *Strategic Management: A Stakeholder Approach*. Pitman Publishing.

Freeman, R. E., & McVea, J. (2001). *A Stakeholder Approach to Strategic Management* (SSRN Scholarly Paper No. ID 263511). Rochester, NY: Social Science Research Network. Retrieved from http://papers.ssrn.com/abstract=263511

Habitat for Humanity International mission statement and principles. Retrieved December 22, 2015, from http://www.habitat.org/how/mission_statement.aspx

Heath, Chip, and Dan Heath. *Decisive – How to Make Better Choices in Life and Work*. New York: Crown Business, 2013.

Humphrey, A. (2005). SWOT analysis for management consulting. *SRI Alumni Newsletter* (SRI International).

Humphrey, A. (2005). The Origin of SWOT Analysis. *European Quality*.

Janis, I. L., & Mann, L. (1977). *Decision making: A psychological analysis of conflict, choice, and commitment.* New York: The Free Press.

Keeney, R. L. (1996). *Value-Focused Thinking: A Path to Creative Decisionmaking.* Harvard University Press.

Keeney, R. L. (1996). Value-focused thinking: Identifying decision opportunities and creating alternatives. *European Journal of Operational Research, 92*(3), 537–549.

Kirkwood, C. W. (1996). *Strategic Decision Making: Multiobjective Decision Analysis with Spreadsheets* (1st ed.). Duxbury Press.

Kiva - About Us. Retrieved December 22, 2015, from http://www.kiva.org/about

O'Neill, J. (2000). SMART Goals, SMART Schools. *Educational Leadership, 57*(5), 46–50.

Olsen, E. G. (2011). *Strategic planning kit for dummies.* Indianapolis, IN: Wiley Publishing, Inc.

Porter, Michael E. *Competitive strategy: Techniques for analyzing industries and competitors.* Simon and Schuster, 2008.

Rubin, R. S. (2002). Will the real SMART goals please stand up. *The Industrial-Organizational Psychologist, 39*(4), 26–27.

Rumelt, Richard P. (2011). *Good Strategy/Bad Strategy.* Crown Business.

Selart, M., & Johansen, S. T. (2011). Understanding the Role of Value☐Focused Thinking in Idea Management. *Creativity and Innovation Management, 20*(3), 196-206.

Sinek, Simon. *Start with Why: How Great Leaders Inspire Everyone to Take Action.* New York: Portfolio, 2009.

Stakeholder Analysis. Retrieved December 22, 2015, from http://www.stakeholdermap.com/stakeholder-analysis.html

Winterfeldt, D. von, & Edwards, W. (1986). *Decision Analysis and Behavioral Research.* Cambridge University Press.

About the Author

Ursina Teuscher has a PhD in psychology and a professional degree (MS) as a career counselor from the University of Freiburg, Switzerland. As a decision coach, consultant and facilitator, she helps individuals and organizations think creatively and systematically about their decisions, and achieve their goals.

Ursina's published research and teaching over the years has focused on cognitive psychology and neuroscience, learning, memory, decision making, and coaching techniques. Her consulting and educational projects include strategic planning for small businesses and non-profit organizations, and post-graduate training courses in decision aiding techniques for career counselors.

She currently teaches Decision Making at Portland State University (PSU), Career and Lifestyle Counseling at Marylhurst University, and Strategic Planning at the CLIMB Center for Advancement in Portland, Oregon.

Other Publications by Ursina Teuscher

Books

Anderson, B., Hahn, D., & Teuscher, U. (2013). *Heart and Mind: Mastering the Art of Decision Making.* CreateSpace Independent Publishing Platform.

Teuscher, U. (2014). *Increasing Personal Productivity in Healthy and Sustainable Ways.* CreateSpace Independent Publishing Platform.

Teuscher, U. (2013). *Workbook: Beating Procrastination 101.* CreateSpace Independent Publishing Platform.

Selected Peer-Reviewed Articles

Misuraca, R., & Teuscher, U. (2013). Time flies when you maximize— Maximizers and satisficers perceive time differently when making decisions. *Acta Psychologica, 143*(2), 176–180.

Misuraca, R., Teuscher, U., & Faraci, P. (2015). Is more choice always worse? Age differences in the overchoice effect. *Journal of Cognitive Psychology, 0*(0), 1–14.

Teuscher, U. (2003a). Evaluation of a decision training program for vocational guidance. *International Journal for Educational and Vocational Guidance, 3*(3), 177–192.

Teuscher, U., & Mitchell, S. H. (2011). Relation between time perspective and delay discounting: a literature review. *The Psychological Record, 61*(4), 7.

Teuscher, U., & Teuscher, C. (2007). Reconsidering the double standard of aging: Effects of gender and sexual orientation on facial attractiveness ratings. *Personality and Individual Differences, 42*(4), 631–639.

More About This Topic

Blog on Decision Making and Goal Achievement

by Ursina Teuscher, PhD

If you're interested in hearing more about decision making, creative and rational thinking, and goal achievement, sign up here: http://www.teuschercoaching.com/blog

Typical blog posts include updates on latest research findings, featured videos or articles, book recommendations, and announcements of news or special events.

Coaching, Facilitation, Courses

by Ursina Teuscher, PhD

Get more information on my website or by contacting me directly: http://www.teuschercoaching.com

www.ingramcontent.com/pod-product-compliance
Lightning Source LLC
Chambersburg PA
CBHW081314170526
45166CB00011B/3526

* 9 7 8 1 5 1 9 2 9 5 9 6 5 *